Family Tree Building Basics:
A Book for Beginners

By Mercedes Brons

First electronic edition, May 2020
First softcover edition, October 2020

Softcover edition:
ISBN: 9798648031562

Table of Contents

A note from the author

    I am so glad that you have decided to learn about the hobby of genealogy. There is no doubt that you will find your ancestors as exciting as I have found mine to be.

    You do not have to be descended from royalty or someone famous to be proud of your family's unique story! Every single person has a rich tapestry of heritage to explore, and genealogy allows us to do just that.

What are the tools needed to build a family tree?

    You only need a few tools to do family tree research. You can use a computer, mobile phone, or tablet to locate documents and keep track of your research. If you do not have those items, a journal or notebook and a pen and access to your local library will suffice.

Finally, you will need to have plenty of curiosity about your ancestors. Of course!

What will you learn in this book?

This book covers the basics of all aspects of genealogy research, including how to take good notes, what type of records you should look for, and how to find your ancestors without spending too much money. Plus, you will learn how to solve those tough family mysteries.

Best of luck in your search for ancestors!

Mercedes

Why You Should Build a Family Tree

CHAPTER ONE

Why You Should Build a Family Tree

You are about to embark on an amazing journey. Genealogy, the study of ancestry and descent, is a rewarding and fulfilling hobby.

You picked up this book because you have just recently gotten serious about building your family tree.

There are many reasons that people hesitate to start building a family tree:

- They worry it will be too difficult

- It sounds boring

- Their cousin already built a tree

- They do not know how to find information

My hope is that after you finish reading the first chapter of this book, you will be inspired to begin building your family tree right away. The rest of the chapters will give you strategies and ideas for how to do it.

With all the advances made possible by technology over the past few decades modern genealogists can confidently agree that everyone can find an aspect of genealogy that fascinates and excites them. It is easier than ever before, and you do not even have to leave your house.

Family tree research is seriously exciting

If you are looking for some excitement, you might be surprised to find out that you can find just about any kind of adrenaline rush you need while hunting down details about your ancestors. Contained within the family tree of just about any family is enough drama for a soap opera, complete with all the plot twists.

Adventure, joy, success, fame, romance, and overwhelming love, meet with heartbreak, tragedy, deceit, murder, illness, theft, and infidelity. All of this is made even more fascinating by the fact that you are researching your own ancestors! It is more than enough to keep almost anyone riveted for hours at a time.

Plus, who does not love a good mystery? I guarantee that you will find plenty of those in your family tree. It is almost like being an amateur detective. Often, I have more puzzles and mysteries than I do hard, cold facts.

Why did my great-great grandmother marry one of her husband's brewery employees after his death? Did this second husband leave and take their son to Germany, never to return?

I may never learn the whole story, but I will have a lot of fun trying.

You can build your family tree for free, right from your living room

There are several particularly good, free places to build your family tree online, so you do not have to worry about having to spend a lot of money downloading expensive software. They are all easy to use, too.

Want to find a scanned image your great-great grandfather's baptismal records in Slovakia? Do you need to see the record of your great-grandfather's purchase of a property in 1899 in Philadelphia? How about a photograph of your great-great-great-great grandfather's grave stone in Vermont?

You can find those, too, totally for free. Really!

There are thousands of volunteers and employees of various organizations all over the world who have worked, and continue to work, tirelessly to scan and index the billions of records available on our ancestors. With a smartphone, tablet, or computer, you can access a sizeable portion of these documents for free, right from home.

There are many hundreds, if not thousands, of websites that you can use to learn about your ancestors. Most of the information available can be located for free.

You might have to take some time to learn how to use the available tools and websites, but this can almost be as much fun as the family tree research itself.

Even if your relative has built a tree, you should build one, too

I have a fairly good friend who I see on a regular occasion. He is elderly and has done a DNA test but has not started building a family tree because he has a cousin who has "already done all of the research." He is missing out on so much; it almost breaks my heart.

Here is his situation:

His first cousin is really a half-first cousin. Typically, first cousins share 50% of their ancestors with their other first cousins on the same side of the family. In the case of a half-first cousin, they share 25% of their ancestors.

My friend's half-first cousin has done good research. I have seen it myself. However, it is only on 25% of my friend's tree.

In other words, his half-first cousin's family tree excludes 75% of *his* ancestors. My friend is missing out on an incredible wealth of information about his ancestors not included in his half-first cousin's research.

If your genealogist-cousin is a second cousin, then you can imagine that the ancestors that you share are fewer still, which makes it even more imperative that you build your own family tree.

What if the person who has started building a tree is your sibling? What better than to be able to share your progress and even aid someone in their research who is just as invested in learning as much about *all* your ancestors as you are?

Genealogy is **NOT** *only* for grandparents

Did you know that genealogy is the second most popular hobby in the United States? It is also the second most popular thing to do online.

I will not mention the first most popular thing... it is, well, ahem, inappropriate for decent company. Those of you with an imagination will probably be able to guess what it is.

I could not find reliable statistics to cite the average age of people doing family tree research. However, young people on social media regularly post about finding an ancestor's birth certificate, or wishing that their young children would nap so they would have more time to work on their family tree.

Personally, I started spending a lot of time on family tree research when I was resting after the birth of my youngest child. I had to sit down to feed him, and I had a free hand to hold my phone to scroll through census records and DNA matches.

After a time, my passing interest became a passionate hobby. I am sure that I was not alone in the under-40 genealogist crowd.

While we may perceive genealogy as being a pastime that only our grandparents and great-grandparents became involved in after their retirement, it is inaccurate. There are many people who have been lifelong fans of their ancestors from a young age.

Having older and more experienced people to turn to for help in our research is also an advantage. So, let us not pre-judge each other because of our ages – young or old.

A family tree can help you better understand your DNA results

If you have already done a DNA test or you think you might take a test in the future, building a family tree is an absolute must for you. Building a family tree will help you get the most from your DNA results by helping you learn from your DNA matches.

One of the most well-known aspects of DNA results is called the "ethnicity estimate", or ancestry composition, which basically tells you where your family most likely lived over the past few hundred years.

By building a family tree before or after you get your DNA results, you will have a better idea as to the accuracy of your ethnicity estimates. However, this is not the most useful aspect of DNA testing.

Many people use their DNA matches to build their family trees further back, using evidence from the trees of their DNA matches and the genetic material you share as additional clues in addition to traditional genealogy documentation.

You can also verify the accuracy of your family tree by checking out your DNA matches. Since your DNA relatives are descended from ancestors that you share, your family trees should reflect this.

How Far Back Can a Tree Go?

CHAPTER TWO

How Far Back Can a Family Tree Go?

If you have been interested in genealogy for a while, you have probably heard someone say that they have traced their ancestry back to William the Conqueror (d. 1087), Julius Caesar (d. 44 BC), or even Adam and Eve.

It is exceedingly easy to poke fun at people who claim that their pedigrees go that far back in history, but it does lead us to wonder: *How far back can we go in genealogy?*

In this chapter, I will discuss the following related topics:

- How far back is it possible to go in genealogy

- Can DNA results help you go back further in history than traditional genealogy?

- Whether all our "ancestors" are really related to us

Most genealogists strive to make sure that our research is accurate, and accuracy is one reasons that many people who are interested in family tree research decide to take DNA tests. Whether or not you think accuracy really matters, it is interesting to ponder how far back you can realistically (and accurately) build a family tree.

How far back can we accurately build our family tree?

While we can build our family trees back as far as we want to, what we really want to know is how far back can we *accurately* build our family trees?

The answer to this question is a concise "it depends." I have multiple lines in my family tree that go back to the 1600s, for example. Some I am surer of than others.

How far back we can really build our trees back depends on many factors including the religion, race, social class, place of birth, culture, and luck of our ancestors. To build our trees, we need documentation and evidence, and whether said documentation and evidence exists depends on some of those factors I just mentioned.

There is also a meaningful discussion to be had about how significant is it to be descended from a particular notable person a thousand years ago. For example, depending on which mathematician you ask, William the Conqueror is likely to have at least a few hundred million descendants.

Is it better to have an exceptionally well-researched family tree going back 6-8 generations where you have a very good understanding of the lives that these recent ancestors lived?

Compared to a dubious family tree going back twenty or more generations, it seems like the former would provide more substance for the formation of our understanding of our family's unique story.

It takes luck to build a family tree hundreds of years back

To be sure, we genealogists like to feel that our research is the result of pure skill.

In order to get evidence for our trees, we need luck. We would be remiss to not admit that luck plays a big part in whether we can build our tree and how far back we are able to go.

In other words, we need some good luck.

Good luck is finding a full-page newspaper article detailing our great-great-great grandfather's life and death. Our ancestors needed to be lucky enough to have the socioeconomic resources to have records created about them, and we need to be lucky enough to look in the right place to find those records.

One of my great-great uncle's birth was not registered with the state at the time of his birth in 1896 because the family had to choose between religious ceremonies or civil registration. They could not afford both.

The records themselves also need to be "lucky" to survive centuries without being damaged. This can also be a function of the economic and political well-being of the places that our ancestors were lucky enough to be born.

Bad luck is what I would call the 1890 US Federal Census records being destroyed in a fire or church records being burned in some of the vengeful, hateful wars we saw in the 20th century.

Family tree records depend on religion

Each religion has different customs of record keeping, and these customs typically vary by country or culture. Sometimes, religious organizations were the only institutions keeping records in a particular area in a given time period, and so religious records would only pertain to those people who practiced that religion.

In some places, however, religious institutions were required to register births and deaths of everyone, even those who did not adhere to their customs or religion.

Religion has also traditionally been an important part in how our ancestors lived their lives. In some places, religion governs social circles and choice of marriage partners.

Understanding how our ancestors interacted with their religion can help us know which records to look for and where they might be. We will also be able to learn more about their wider influences to gain more insight into their lives.

Even in modern times, genealogists find themselves depending on religious institutions for research and documentation purposes. For example, one of my favorite genealogy research sites, *Family Search* (familysearch.org), is connected with its parent organization, the *Church of Jesus Christ of Latter-Day Saints*.

The wealth or fame of our ancestors affects how much we can learn about them

Even though written records of events like births and deaths of "regular people" have been kept in some places for hundreds of years, not every birth and death was recorded in places where records were kept.

The race, social class, or socioeconomic status of a person had a lot to do with whether or not important events in their lives were recorded in an official manner, or whether society in general felt that it was important to document noteworthy aspects of their lives.

An extreme example? If our 10th great-grandfather was the King of England, we are more likely to find out lots of details about his life than we would if he were the servant cleaning the king's bedchambers.

How many books do you think have been written about the guy cleaning the king's bedchambers versus the king?

Even without this extreme example that probably does not apply to many of us, we can find lots of instances in our family trees of people with different backgrounds being "remembered" by historical records in different ways.

In my own research, I have found an endless supply of records about my great-great grandparents on my paternal grandmother's side. Quite literally, I could seemingly research forever and continue to find tiny newspaper clippings on these ancestors because of their position and involvement in their local community.

On my maternal grandmother's side of the family, my great-great grandmother's humble Polish origins and migration to the US was notable to almost no one, as the lack of records pertaining to her has continued to show.

One of the best things about family tree research, however, is that we can never really know what we will find until we start to look. We do not know if we had notable people in our tree who will be easily researched until we build our tree back far enough to find them.

Finally, I feel it is especially worthwhile to research those ancestors who were overlooked by their community and larger society. In our own way, we honor those ancestors by researching their lives and understanding them in a way that they may not have been understood during their lifetime.

How far back can the average person trace their family tree?

As you can see, how far we can accurately build our tree back really does depend on a lot of different factors.

Most people will be able to trace all lines of their family tree back to the 1800s, assuming they begin with the names of their parents and grandparents. Some people might be able to build certain lines of their family tree back to the 1600s.

Few people might be able to trace a few lines of their tree back further than about the year 1600. Usually, trees that go this far back are unreliable, unless a person has a very notable person in their family tree that has had a lot of independent research done about them.

It would be considered highly unusual for someone to be able to trace their family tree back as far as 1400. Most serious genealogists would view a tree that goes back to the year 1400 with a large dose of skepticism.

There are some exceptions to this generalization, however. For example, the Icelandic culture is famous for its detailed genealogies.

It is said that "everyone" in Iceland knows their genealogy, and amazingly some Icelanders can trace their ancestry back as many as 30 generations! This is due to a project called The Book of Icelanders (*Íslendingabók),* which attempts to document the genealogy of every Icelander, using formal and informal censuses from hundreds of years ago as a base of information.

Can DNA help you go back further than traditional genealogy?

DNA testing is excellent for assisting in breaking down brick walls in your tree closer than about 6-8 generations ago, but it will not be much help in figuring out who your 11th great-grandmother's biological father really was.

I like to suggest that DNA testing can help us absolutely verify our recent ancestry and can help us feel sure about our ancestry going back about 6-8 generations.

Even though DNA testing cannot help us go further back in our family tree than traditional genealogy can, it does help build our tree's foundation. I would hate to spend years researching my family tree only to later find out that I had the wrong great-great-great grandfather in one line of my tree.

That would mean that all the ancestors that I included for my great-great-great grandfather were incorrect. Depending on how many generations I included after him, it could result in many years of wasted research.

Once I am sure about all my recent ancestors, I can spend time building my tree farther back and feel more confident about its accuracy.

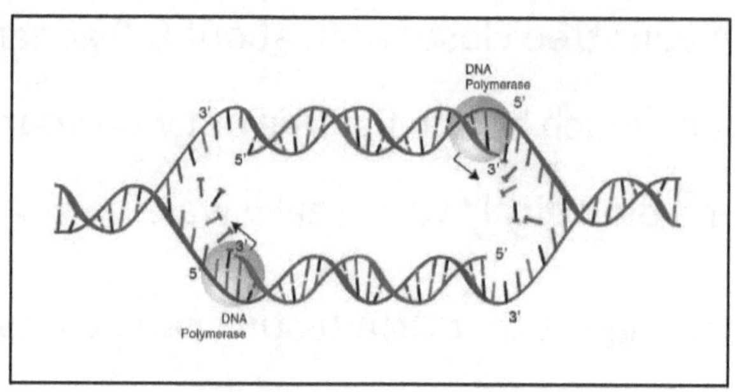

DNA Testing is an excellent way to learn more about your ancestry, and it can be a lot of fun, too.

Image Credit: National Human Genome Research

Some of our ancestors are not really related to us

One important aspect of accuracy in a family tree is the occurrence of "non-paternity events." Every once in a while, a father unknowingly raises a child who is not biologically related to him. This is rare but does occur in about 1 out of 100 births, on average. It happens more in some cultures than others and has been more common in certain time periods than others.

This means that if you consider that we have about 1000 8th great-grandparents, meaning that there were about 500 marriages that took place among that generation of your ancestors. This could mean that as many of five of your great-great-great-great-great-great-great grandparents have the "wrong" father listed on their birth record or church record.

On other occasions, a father *does* know that the child is not his biologically, but he decides to help raise the baby anyway. Sometimes, these events are not recorded anywhere.

My paternal grandfather's favorite aunt was not biologically descended from her father, my great-great grandfather. This was revealed to me through my father's DNA results, as he only shared about half of the expected amount of DNA with his grand-aunt's grandchildren.

The rest of the family seems unaware of this, however. There are dozens of family trees online who list my grandfather's aunt's father as my great-great grandfather. These stories are common in families.

While I cannot tell you for sure whether this happened in your family, I can tell you that it is highly likely that it happened at least once at some point. How often it happened would depend on your family's history.

While DNA testing can help sort some of this out, we can safely assume that everyone who has a large family tree has a "wrong" person (or several) in their tree somewhere. This is true even in the "best" of families!

What are Genealogy Records?

CHAPTER THREE

What are Genealogy Records

For those new to family tree research, you will want to know what genealogical records are. In this chapter, I will discuss the definition of genealogy records, as well as explain the best records to look for and where to find them.

Even those of you who have gotten your feet wet in family tree research might find ideas and inspiration on where to look for documents in this section of the book.

Genealogy records, used to illustrate one person's familial relationship to another, are the fundamental building blocks of family tree research. Information from genealogy records is often presented in the form of formal pedigree charts, family trees, or even written narratives.

Many people think of genealogy records as only those records that serve to document when and where a person lived, as well as who is descended from that person and who they are descended from.

In reality, genealogy records can be used for so much more. Those passionate for genealogy research will use genealogical records to document as much about an ancestor's life as possible, including their lifestyle and why they made the choices that they did.

What type of genealogy records should I look for?

When I first became interested in learning more about my family tree many years ago, I had no idea what types of records I might be able to find that could help me with my research. Most importantly, I had no idea of the depth of information that I would be able to learn about my ancestors.

There are many dozens of types of records and documents that can be located pertaining to your ancestors or historical people. In fact, I have been able to learn so much about certain ancestors in my family tree that I almost feel like I could sit down at a table with them as someone who knows them personally. They would likely be shocked about how much I have been able to learn about them.

I wonder what kind of amazing information you will be able to learn about your ancestors?

What kind of genealogy records are there?

Here are more than 20 categories of records that you can explore to learn about people who lived before us:

- Census records (usually done at regular intervals)

- Vital records (like birth, marriage death records)

- Church records

- Court records

- Oral histories

- Professional or occupational records

- Historical newspapers

- Family Bibles

- Land records (often held at the local or state administrative level)

- Military records

- Academic records

- Financial records (bank and tax records)

- Historical accounts printed in books

- City directories (like old phone books!)

- Obituaries (both in print and modern online obituaries)

- Immigration records, including travel records (like ship passenger lists and passports)

- Voter lists

- Photographic evidence

- Personal journals and diaries

- Published family trees and pedigrees (including online)

- Cemetery records

There are likely dozens more categories of genealogy records. I am regularly surprised at the creativity of how genealogists can locate records.

As you can see, there are many potential sources of information about our ancestors. With a little time, dedication, and a sprinkling of luck, we can put together a relatively complete view of what their lives may have been like.

All of this gives me pause, occasionally. I wonder what type of records I am leaving behind for my distant descendants to help track down information about my life.

How can I find genealogy records?

If you took a good glance at the previous list of types of genealogy records, you might not be surprised to know that you can find helpful records in many different places. You will be able to find lots of genealogy documents online, but more traditional research might be required to locate offline genealogy records.

There are many amazing websites that have made billions of records available (i.e. digitized and searchable) for those of us who would prefer to stay at home and peruse records online. Some of these websites are free, and others require a subscription to access.

My go-to sites for accessing genealogy records?

- Ancestry

- Family Search

- Newspapers.com

Do not limit yourself to only the big sites in genealogical records, however. You can often find online records pertaining to your ancestor at the state and local level.

For example, I was able to locate property records from the 1890's for my great-great grandfather on a Philadelphia city site. If you know where your ancestor lived, you can see if the local or state government allows access to records on their website.

Eventually, even the most skilled internet sleuths are required to hop into the car and visit courthouses or state archives to do research the "old fashioned" way. Not everything is available online, and the records that you can find in person are often the most valuable in solving some of our tough family history mysteries.

I have tried to combine vacations or other travel with genealogy record searches. It is not feasible for everyone, of course, but if you spot an opportunity to do so, I would recommend it.

For instance, I was plotting my drive from the Newark, NJ area to my home, a 14 hour drive, when I realized that my route was going to take me almost directly past the church where my great-great uncle was baptized. I had been trying to solve the mystery of the origins of my great-great grandmother for years, and I thought that the church might still have records from his baptism in 1896.

Sure enough, they did, indeed. The church secretary went into a separate room and retrieved an old, leather-bound book. She even let me take a photograph of the original baptismal record from 1896 and it took me a little closer to solving my mystery.

Plus, it was an amazing feeling to walk into a place that my great-great grandmother had been in to baptize her son on Christmas Day. The original church building, built more than 130 years ago, is still standing.

Lingering in the doorway of the church, I tried to put myself in her shoes. I was standing where she had once stood holding her newborn son.

I took time to explore the cemetery to look for surnames that might be connected to my family and wondered if she had ever taken those same steps.

I had to travel to make some of my discoveries. If you are lucky enough to live in the same geographic area as your ancestors, you should explore the local opportunities for research. Local newspapers and courthouses are often a goldmine for genealogical records because you cannot always find similar information on the internet.

How To Take Genealogy Notes

CHAPTER FOUR

How to Take Genealogy Notes

You are eager to begin your research, and we are almost to that point. However, I truly want you to get off to a great start in your family tree research by taking excellent genealogy notes right from the start. This is such an important step in doing genealogical research, and while it does not seem exciting initially, you will soon discover how much it can help you.

I do not want you to skip over these important aspects of research, which is a mistake that I made. These mistakes cost me time and money. Plus, my mistakes hurt the quality of my family tree. Taking good notes can save you time in the future and help keep your research focused.

In this chapter, you will learn the best way to take genealogy notes. Plus, I will explain why it is important to take notes of your daily research even if you do not find what you are looking for that day.

Why take genealogy notes?

My great-great grandmother and her daughter-in-law, my great-grandmother, were huge fans of genealogy. They spent lots of time studying, reading and researching our family lines.

Today, I have beautiful pedigrees and some nice family stories written based on their research. What I do not have are their notes.

I found myself wishing that I could read back through their old notes and find out how they came to their conclusions. Additionally, it would be amazing to know exactly where they did and did not look for records. Those missing notes would have helped me discover how I could have filled in some of the blanks in their research.

Since I do not have their notes, I am sure that I have spent a lot of time duplicating their work. While it is good to double-check the research of other genealogists, it would still save me time to know more about the research I am double-checking.

After discovering how important those missing notes were, I realized that I could improve the way I was taking notes and practice better organization. If I am honest, I know that I've spent time looking for a particular record multiple times in the same repository because I forgot that I had already checked and it was not there.

To summarize, taking (good) genealogy notes can help you:

- Avoid forgetting important details

- Save time in the future by not having to repeat things you have already done

- Help you focus your future research by keeping track of thoughts and ideas about what to do next

- If you are working with a family member research-partner, you can work more efficiently by sharing your notes

Plus, would not it be amazing if your great-great grandchild could read through your genealogy notes someday and pick up where you left off?

I do not know if any of my great-great grandchildren will be interested in genealogy, but a girl can dream, right?

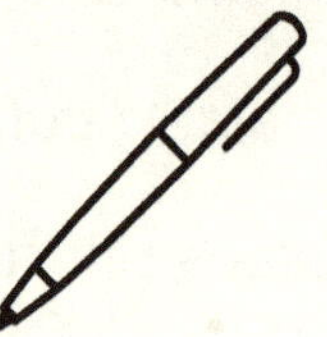

Where to take genealogy notes?

Family tree researchers have lots of options when it comes to taking notes about their research. Some people love using technology and others prefer handwritten notes.

For those who love technology, a simple Microsoft Word or Google Docs file is sufficient. Others use spreadsheets.

Personally, I love journals and notebooks. Nothing compares to the feeling of an actual book of notes.

I put my method of keeping genealogy notes into journal format, called the "Genealogist's Research Journal", which you can find on Amazon. There are more than two hundred pages in the journal – space for lots of daily research entries.

Of course, you can use any method of keeping notes that appeals to you.

Write neatly

This should go without saying, of course, but it is necessary to mention. Your writing should be as legible as possible. Remember, you do not know how long from now you might need to refer to these notes and you might not remember what you were thinking at the time. By writing neatly, you will save yourself (and maybe others in the future) time and frustration.

It can be very confusing to try to work out details about what you were trying to write years after you made the initial entry in your research log. Much confusion can be avoided by neat handwriting.

Include full name and full date of person (or people) who the record is about

Even though it might seem boring to write out a full name or date related to a record that you have found, you should always do it. Avoid using initials or just the last two years of a date.

When researching ancestors from a long time ago, the year becomes especially important. For example, if you say that someone was born in '36, most people will think 1936.

In reality, the date might actually be 1836, 1736 or even 1636. So, use the full year. I promise you will thank yourself.

Do not use unique abbreviations

When I was in college, I worked as a server in a restaurant. The restaurant had specific abbreviations that we had to use when we wrote down a customer's orders.

Does G/OM/CFC mean anything to you? That is an example of the "language" created by the restaurant company that I worked for. The "G" stood for the name of a particular breakfast. "OM" was for eggs, over-medium. And CFC stood for "country fried-chicken".

We were trained thoroughly in using these abbreviations so that way anyone else in the entire restaurant could easily read what we wrote and avoid mistakes. Any cook could cook the meal, and any server could ring the customer up so they could pay for the exact food that they consumed.

Fortunately, we genealogists do not need to make up a new language or new abbreviations to do our research.

We are lucky that the English language (or whichever language that you speak) has already been invented for us and we do not need to use creative abbreviations, expressions, etc. in order to communicate with each other.

When we take genealogy notes, we should *not* get creative and come up with shorthand words to save time or space. Remember, we want other people, including our future selves, to be able to read what we wrote at any time in the future.

Do not change spelling or information from original record

Have you ever found a record that *almost* matches your ancestor? If you think that the record really relates to your ancestor, but the spelling or date is just not quite right, it is okay to allow it into your notes.

However, it is important to retain the original information from the record. This means that you should not change the spelling, dates, locations from the record in order to make it better match to what you already know about your target ancestor.

For example, let us say we are researching Johnathon Swift, born June 11, 1810 in Winchester, Massachusetts. If we find a record for a Johnathon Swift, born February 11, 1810 in Winchester, Massachusetts, it might truly pertain to our ancestor. Maybe the June date is wrong and was mistakenly copied onto a document somewhere.

Alternatively, maybe the February date was entered incorrectly when the index for the documents was created.

Either way, when we take notes about this record, we should document the date discrepancy. We might not really know which date Johnathon was born. In theory, there could have been two people named Johnathon Switft born months apart in the same town. Think: cousins, children of brothers with the same last name.

The same is true for spellings that are different, or birth records that list different parents, or different birth locations. Even if we think we know the correct information, we should always document the actual details included in the source we are recording in our notes.

Record all details about source

Make sure that you include as many details in your notes from the original document as possible. As you might know, even the most seemingly insignificant detail can help you crack family tree mysteries. By including every detail from the source you have discovered, you will get more ideas and do better future research.

For example, I recently realized that I had overlooked an important detail from a passenger manifest pertaining to my ancestor. On the original record, it lists the address that she was planning to reside at in the United States.

I had not written down this detail and only noticed the address while taking a second and third look at the document. Once I realized the address of where she would be staying, I was able to research other residents of the property, figure out their relationship to her, and move on to my next research question. Revisiting previous research is a strategy that I recommend for those who are stuck on an ancestor.

In addition to my previous oversight, I had overlooked that she may have been traveling with another passenger who listed her son's uncle as their brother-in-law. Details like these, even though they are not directly related to our ancestor, can help us make important discoveries.

Include theories, ideas and conclusions

It is a good idea to include ideas or theories that you have in your genealogy notes, but make sure that they are identified as such. Sometimes, we can make educated "guesses" in genealogy and be correct, and so it is good to write down what those guesses are.

I like to include a section in my notes for this type of information because I often get ideas about an ancestor when I am in the midst of researching them. If I write them down, I can come back to them later and see if my idea pans out. Sometimes they do and sometimes they do not, but if you write them down, you will always have a record of the things that you have already tried.

> **REMEMBER**
>
> - Writing down conclusions helps you remember what to do next
> - It's okay to guess in genealogy, as long as you follow it up with research

To keep focused, include "next steps"

Because of my busy schedule, I often run out of time to keep researching. There is always "one more place to search" in genealogy, and I like to write this down before I conclude my research for the day.

Life happens, even to us genealogists!

I write down the next steps so the next time I am researching that ancestor, I can pick up right where I left off and search that next index, website, repository, or whatever it might be.

Building a Family Tree: First Steps

CHAPTER FIVE

Building a Family Tree: First Steps

Are you ready to start building your tree? Genealogy is such a fun adventure, and you have made the first step to getting started: deciding that you want to build a family tree.

In this chapter, you will learn:

- How to choose a platform on which to build a family tree
- Beginning steps to building a tree
- Where to find records and documents about your ancestors
- Tips and tricks to build your tree further back

When I first got started in genealogy, I had no idea how to build a family tree. I had only seen pedigree charts that my older relatives had compiled, and had never considered getting involved in the hobby myself.

It has turned out to be a wonderful experience. I have learned so much about my ancestors and have become the go-to person in the family for all family history related questions.

Where should you build a family tree?

There are lots of places online where you can build a family tree. It is best to build your tree on a website where you can access it wherever you are. If possible, try to build your tree on a platform that allows you to access it from a desktop computer, smartphone, or tablet.

Some of the most popular places to build a tree online:

- **Recommended**: Ancestry (ancestry.com)
- Family Search (familysearch.org) Note: your tree will not be private and that others will be able to edit it
- WikiTree (wikitree.com)

My favorite place to build a family tree is Ancestry. One of the reasons that I prefer Ancestry over many of the other sites for building trees is because I also tested my DNA on the site. Ancestry is free to use to build a family tree, but you do need to have a subscription to get access to most of the records on the site.

By connecting my DNA results to my family tree, I can access a lot of additional features.

There are also some software programs that you can download to build your tree on your computer (i.e. not keep it online). If you prefer this option, you might be interested in Roots Magic, Family Tree Maker, and Legacy.

I have used Legacy personally and found it an adequate and affordable alternative to keeping my tree online. Even so, I still prefer keeping my trees online because I can work on my tree from anywhere as long as I have internet access.

What are the first steps to building a family tree?

Once you have decided to build a family tree and you know where you'd like to build it, you are now ready to start thinking about where you'll get the information you need to start adding people to your tree.

While doing research, it is important to take good genealogy notes. I would recommend keeping your notes in a notebook or journal, as mentioned in the previous chapter.

Your immediate and extended family can provide information about your family tree

Most people quickly jump to online sources of records, but there is one thing that I would like to recommend that you do before you start looking in internet databases.

Talk to your parents, aunts, uncles, cousins, grandparents (or even great-grandparents, if you can), and siblings of your grandparents.

During your conversations with these family members:

- Take notes
- Ask for copies of documents (like marriage, birth, or baptismal certificates) pertaining to your ancestors
- Inquire about photographs of your ancestors

You might be surprised at what you learn!

To complete this step, make sure you add all the immediate and extended family members that you know about/learn about to your family tree. Do not forget to add the details that you learned from these interviews to your tree.

Try to locate your ancestors in all US Federal and state census documents

Once you get the basic people added to your tree (like your mom, dad, grandparents, even great-grandparents), you will want to start looking for documents pertaining to the previous generations of ancestors.

My favorite starting place to look for documents is the US Federal Census. It is a relatively objective collection of information that was taken at regular intervals, and as such is very valuable to genealogists, especially budding genealogists like us.

The most recent Federal Census available for public use online is the 1940 US Federal Census. If your grandparents or great-grandparents were born before then and lived in the US, then you will probably be able to locate their nuclear family in this collection of documents.

Even if you already know a lot about your grandparents or great-grandparents, locating their family on the 1940 Federal Census is going to be the best place to start.

Pay careful attention to each detail reported to see if it lines up with what you know. If you do not know anything, then this information will help you know where to look for additional documents. For example, from the 1940 Census, you can learn whether or not your grandparent lived with their parents in a home that they rented or owned. If they owned their home, then you know that you might be able to look for property records in that county/town pertaining to your ancestors.

Every census document typically reports the names of all the members of the household and their place of birth. By determining each person's relationship to your ancestor, you can add them to your tree and discover new information.

In addition to this, since everyone's place of birth is listed, you now know where you should look to find records. You might find new information that you never would have known.

For example, if your grandparent was born in Ohio and your great-grandparents were born in New York, you might not know that your great-grandparents lived in Pennsylvania for a time. This might have been where your grandparent's older brother was born, and you could learn this detail – and more - from the 1940 Census record. Every little detail, no matter how small, can provide a good clue as to where to look for more documents or records.

The US has taken a census every ten years since 1790, but you will probably find that the most helpful records are from 1850 through 1940. So, make sure to trace your family back through history by locating them and their ancestors in every census record available.

Fill in the story about people in your tree with additional supporting documents

Once you have filled in the basic generations of your tree, you can now focus on finding supporting documents to support (or dispute) what you learned from census records. While census records are an important source of information, they are not always accurate.

For example, when a census taker visited a residence and no one was home, they may have spoken with a neighbor. This is just one example of how inaccurate information ended up on census forms. How many of your neighbors could accurately tell a census taker the names, ages, and places of birth of everyone who lives in your house? If a census taker talked to my neighbors, I have no idea what they might say, but I do know that it would not be 100% accurate.

We need to find evidence in the form of supporting documents to support or dispute what we learn from census records. Supporting documents might come in the form of birth, marriage, and death records, state census documents, property and tax records, court documents, wills, employment records, and even newspaper clippings.

Just like with the census records, pay attention to every detail and record it. If it does not match what you learned from another source, still take note of it. Eventually, you will find enough evidence to help you determine what you feel is the truth.

You can also look to other people's family trees online for clues about your ancestors, but I recommend only using other's trees for guidance. Someone else's family tree would not count as a supporting document or evidence for your tree (more on this below), but it can help you figure out where you might need to look to find evidence.

Add generations in your tree slowly

When most people get started with family tree building, they find themselves focused on building their tree back as far as they can as quickly as they can, typically only adding names and basic information to their tree.

This is called "name collecting" and we do not want to be name collectors. We want to learn complete stories about our ancestors, and so therefore I advise people to go slowly and collect as much information as they can about each ancestor.

Moving too quickly can cause errors, and errors can cause us to add dozens of people to our tree who are not even related to us at all. By moving slowly and carefully, we will save ourselves more headache in the future.

REMEMBER

- Don't be in a rush to add more generations
- Adding people too quickly results in errors

Be careful of information obtained from public family trees online

As I mentioned previously, finding information on other people's family trees can often provide clues, but it is important to be cautious about using unverified information from someone else's tree.

Since you do not know how careful they are about their research, you want to be sure not to copy a mistake from their tree. You can eliminate some potential for error by only using information from family trees that include the sources for the details cited. However, even when a family tree includes a source, we do not know how accurate the source is, or whether or not the record used as a source truly belongs to the ancestor we are researching.

Some family trees even use other family trees as their primary form of sources. This is a huge concern and can create a cycle of misinformation about a pedigree line. Therefore, I always recommend verifying information that you learn from someone else on your own.

Family trees found online can often be used as "clues" to help us direct our research, but they can also be a harmful distraction to our research. Use these family trees wisely.

How to find records and documents to build your tree

You might be surprised at what type of information you will be able to learn about your ancestors.

The clues that you need to figure out who your ancestors were and where they came from are contained within birth, marriage and death records, census documents, church records, city directories, property records, newspapers, school yearbooks, online photographs, and public family trees.

Sometimes we must pay for access to these records, and other times we do not. The following is a list of a few places that you can check to find documents relating to your ancestors.

- Family Search (free records, required to create a free account
- Ancestry (has lots of indexes that are not available anywhere else)
- Find My Past (best for UK records)
- My Heritage

I have included many other strategies and locations for finding genealogy records listed in this book – and do not forget to do a simple Google search for your ancestor. You never know what your search will turn up!

Beginning Research Tips

CHAPTER SIX

Beginning Research Tips

Since you are brand-new to the hobby of genealogy, this list of family tree research tips for beginners will save you time and money. Plus, following these tips will help you learn even more about your family tree. What is not to love?

In this chapter, you'll learn why it is important to talk to your family members, as well as:

- Whether you should get a genealogy site subscription right away

- How to keep your research organized

- Why you should never guess when it comes to genealogy

- And more!

Talk to your older family members about family history

My number one tip for genealogy beginners is to not overlook your most valuable resource of family tree information. By conducting informal interviews or conversations with these relatives, you can learn important details about your family that can help you determine future research areas and even strategy.

Believe it or not, this was something that I first overlooked when I got started. Instead of starting with my living relatives, I spent lots of time poring over documents and records learning information that could have easily been uncovered in a ten minute telephone call.

Which relatives are best to talk to? Talk to as many of the following relatives as you can locate, either on the phone, in person, or via letter or e-mail:

- Parents
- Aunts/Uncles
- Grandparents

- Great-grandparents

- Siblings of your grandparents or great-grandparents

- Older first and second cousins

- If none of the above are available, older siblings can also be a good source of information, as they may know family history that you are not aware of

I cannot stress the importance of this tip enough. While researching more distant ancestors might seem more exciting, you will have a more accurate family tree with more context if you start your research with those closest to you.

In my own research, I have learned details by speaking with relatives that I never would have discovered by searching through genealogical records. When my grandmother learned that I was interested in family history, she began to tell me stories about her life and ancestors each time we spoke on the telephone. This is how I learned that her grandfather, an Illinois native, owned a small goldmine in Colorado during the time he spent out west trying to make his fortune.

Learning about his gold mine in Colorado helped me understand why I had found a marriage record for him in a small Colorado town. His second wife was from Colorado, too, which had also previously confused me.

Going through the process of conducting family interviews is also an excellent way to document your family's living history. The notes that you take can be compiled into a valuable record for future generations.

In order to develop this list, I examined my own experience as a genealogist. I made a ton of mistakes when I first got started, and ideas like the ones I include below would have saved me a lot of frustration.

When I first started researching, I did not take myself seriously as a genealogist. I thought that taking genealogy notes was something that only professional, serious researchers did. I was mistaken. Taking good genealogy notes is something that is a crucial learning tool for people who are just beginning their family tree research. If I had taken better notes sooner, I would have saved myself many (many!) hours of frustration and would have done faster and more efficient research.

If you need a refresher on genealogy note taking, please refer to chapter four of this book.

REMEMBER

- Your relatives are the best source of information about your family
- Take notes when you talk to your relatives about the family tree

Do not rush to get subscriptions to family tree research sites

When I talk to people who are interested in researching their family tree, one of the first questions they ask is which site they should get a subscription to. The answer is quite simple: If you have not yet really started your research, do not get any subscriptions.

Subscriptions to any family tree research or genealogy site can be on the pricey side. This means that you want to be sure that you have formed your research strategy before you decide which site you should subscribe to, if any.

There are lots of great places to research your ancestors for free, too.

Once you know for sure what you need to learn, you can research the top sites to see which ones make the most sense to subscribe to.

Pick an online site to host your family tree

There are many great (and free!) places to build and host your family tree. I highly recommend using a site like Ancestry, or similar site, to build your tree for free. If you have your family tree stored online, you can access it from anywhere. Plus, if anything ever happens to your computer, all your family tree work is saved in the cloud for you access later on.

I did not know anything about genealogy software when I first got interested in genealogy, so I just picked the first thing that showed up in my Google search. Fortunately, it was a good choice; I went with Ancestry since it is free and easy. In my case, it was luck. If you have not decided, my suggestion is to try a few out to see which you like the best.

Most websites allow you to download your family tree into the GEDCOM file format. This is great for having a backup on your computer or if you decide you want to continue your research somewhere else, like on another platform.

Make sure your family tree research stays organized

No matter how or where you decide to build your family tree, you should always have some sort of system for organizing the information that you learn.

I cannot remember how many times I have spent time researching a fact that I had already learned before. This sounds silly, but it is true. This happens most often when I start working on an ancestor that I have not spent much time on in a long time.

For example, just last night, I was researching one of my 64 great-great-great-great grandparents. Before I could learn something new about him, I had to re-familiarize myself with what I already knew. Then, I could figure out what I needed to learn. This is one reason that I like Ancestry – all my records, documents, pictures, and facts are all on his profile for easy access.

Do not be like I was when I first started. If you take notes, keep them organized and add them to your family tree, you will save lots of time.

Take a DNA test to see what you learn about your family's origins

If you really want to jump headfirst into genealogy, why not take a DNA test and learn how you can use DNA for genealogy? DNA testing is a great way to verify the accuracy of your family tree, and your DNA matches can help you learn more about your ancestors.

While I have had always been mildly interested in genealogy, the true passion for it began after I took a DNA test. DNA testing began an amazing journey.

Whether you want to learn the origins of your maternal or paternal lines, find biological family, or discover new ancestors, DNA testing will surely be one of your most valuable and favorite family tree research tools.

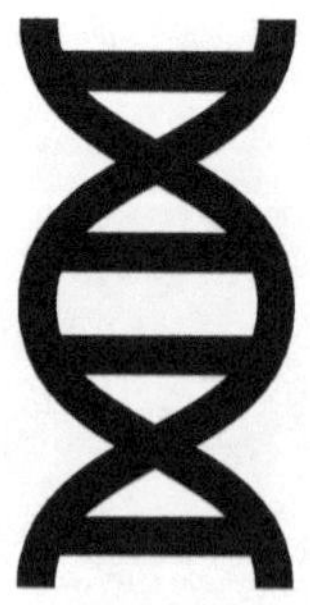

Never guess when it comes to your family tree

In one of the previous sections of this chapter, I mentioned that I was working on one of my 4th great-grandparents last night. His name is Samuel Butler, and he was born in Ohio in about 1821.

My great-grandmother had spent many years of her life doing genealogy research for both her lines and those of her husband. Using DNA and genealogy, I have gone back through her work to verify each ancestor. However, there is one spot in the pedigrees where she hit a brick wall. I figured that since this ancestor was not too far back in history, I should be able to easily find some records showing who Samuel's parents were.

Nope! Nothing. I am beginning to believe that there are no records pertaining to Samuel's birth.

There are lots of public family trees online, however, whose owners seem to believe they know who Samuel's parents are. There are parents listed for Samuel in most people's trees on the site.

I assume that someone "guessed." The problem is that there is no evidence that the couple included as Samuel's parents on most public family trees ever lived in Ohio, even if the genealogists who built those trees believed it to be the case. Every record pertaining to the couple puts them firmly and permanently in the Northeast US.

So, how was Samuel born in Ohio if his parents never lived there? The answer is probably that these people are NOT his parents. Imagine if I had spent the next few years of my life researching the wrong people and adding their ancestors to my family tree? While there are certainly worse fates, it is not ideal.

Do not depend on other people's family tree research – it might be wrong

There is a lot of incorrect information out there in the wide world. Genealogy is no exception. If we depend only on what we are told by others, we can get in lots of trouble.

> **REMEMBER**
>
> - Online trees are a big source of the spread of inaccurate family tree information
> - Always double-check information gathered from other genealogists

We should not blindly follow information printed in family trees that we might find online, or even books of pedigrees that have been published by professionals. Instead, we should carefully use the research of others.

I like to think of family trees and similar records as suggestions, a loose guide to help me form my research hypothesis. Vital records, as well as other types of genealogical records, can help me determine for myself whether I will put someone in my tree.

If I add the incorrect ancestors for Samuel to my tree, then even more people will assume that these ancestors are correct and I will likely be aiding the spread of misinformation about our family line.

Build your family tree "wide" for best results

The aspect of research that gets most people excited is getting "further back" on their family tree. This means that the focus is on only finding the ancestors of your ancestors, working back in a straight line.

My suggestion is that we should not do that. Instead, I recommend building a "wide" family tree in order to learn as much as we can about our broader family.

A wide family tree includes the siblings of your ancestors, and their spouses and children, at the very least. Some people add a few generations of the descendants of their ancestors' siblings, too.

What is the benefit of building a wide tree?

Apart from simply knowing more about where your relatives lived, or still live, you will also more easily find information about your ancestors. For example, maybe one or both of the parents of your ancestor went to live with one of your ancestor's siblings

Maybe one or more of your ancestor's siblings went through the process to become a naturalized citizen, and that would enable you to find the name of the town in their home country where they were born. Perhaps your ancestor's sibling is the reason that your ancestor moved from one location to another.

These are just a few of the many situations that I have encountered in my own family tree. What will you find about your ancestors by building your tree wide?

Consider doing "offline" family tree research when you have the opportunity

There are billions of digital records available online, but sometimes they are not the records that we really need to move us forward in our research. This means that we will, occasionally, need to move out from behind our computers and actually go somewhere to find a document.

Does this sound intimidating? Doing research in person is easier than you might think. Plus, you will meet interesting people and feel like a true family tree detective.

Plan your family tree research to save time

Do not approach your family tree in a haphazard manner. Instead, decide your research strategy in advance and work on the same line of your tree during your research sessions.

Have you ever heard the saying, "plan the work and work the plan"? Well, it is true for family tree research, too!

I recommend working in "batches." This means, for example, that when I sit down to research my Samuel Butler ancestor, I should focus on him, his parents, his children, etc.

I should not work on him for a little while and then switch to a completely different line of my family where the records are not even in the same language. I will waste time having to orient myself each time I switch back and forth between lines.

Yes, every genealogist, no matter how experienced, gets distracted in their research and suddenly veers off their plan when they see something interesting that reminds them of another ancestor they want to know more about. If you can avoid this occurring too many times, you will save yourself a lot of time.

Strategies for Building a Bigger Tree

CHAPTER SEVEN

Strategies for Building a Bigger Tree

There are many things that we can do to learn more about our ancestors and their families and build a bigger, better family tree.

A big family tree does not only include your recent ancestors. Your big tree will also contain information about cousins – even distant ones.

With the right techniques and some dedication, your family tree can extend many generations into the past. Believe it or not, building the "wide" tree is exactly how you achieve this goal.

In this chapter, discover some easy strategies that will help you add more people to your tree. More importantly, they will expand your understanding of your family's journey throughout history.

Let us get started, shall we?

Listen to family stories

There is so much written out there about how many times family stories are not true. Especially with the advent of DNA testing, it is easier than ever to prove or disprove long-held family beliefs.

I had an interesting experience, however, that I would like to share here. There is value to talking with older relatives and listening to those family stories because sometimes there is truth to them.

Our family stories can sometimes lead us to discover something completely surprising about our heritage. Occasionally, we be able to find out whether the story was true, or whether it was fabricated. If we are lucky, we might be able to learn what inspired the story. And sometimes, we learn something really, really sad, which is what I learned during my exploration of a story I was told about a year ago.

Talk to your oldest relatives and hear their stories

I have been spending a lot of time lately researching my great-great-great grandfather. His father's name was Anton Reitz, who was born in Germany about 1844. About a year ago, I was able to speak with an elderly cousin who is Anton Reitz' great-grandson. My elderly cousin is one of my late grandmother's oldest first cousins, and while he never met Anton Reitz, he did know Anton's youngest son.

Anton's youngest son, Charles, never met his father because he died before he was born, but he did remember stories that he was told about him growing up. And I was grateful that Charles told his grandson some of those stories, and that his grandson, Richard, was able to relay those to me.

Imagine, a family story passed down from the 1880s and being repeated in 2018! It is a family story more 130 years old, which to me is incredible – true or not.

Make sure you take notes when older relatives tell you stories

My biggest regret when I spoke with my cousin was that I did not have anything to write with. No pencil, no paper, not even a stick of eyeliner to scrawl down a name or a date. I tried as hard as I could to remember everything that he told me. There is one particular bit of information that he gave to me that I thought was interesting.

Richard relayed to me that Anton was married when he left Germany and that he had had a family there. I am not sure exactly what Anton said to Charles, but I do know that Richard's dad and maybe even Richard put their own spin on the story. Maybe they added more details to make it make sense, or make it mean what they wanted it to mean.

Basically, the family belief was that Anton had left his wife and children behind in Germany and had come to the United States by himself, and that we had cousins – descended from Anton – who were living in Germany, perhaps living today. Even by today's standards, it is kind of scandalous to imagine that my great-great-great grandfather abandoned his wife and kids in Germany and left them to fend for themselves, and that he just remarried in the US and had a brand-new family, forgetting his old life completely.

An old family story might only have an element of truth to it

The story that I just told you would absolutely be scandalous if it were true. And if it were true, or if I believed it to be true, it could send me on a wild goose chase searching for the descendants of my great-great-great grandfather, Anton Reitz, who might still live in Germany. Anton's German-born great-grandchildren, if they existed, would be my parent's second cousins once-removed.

And by the way, I know that life is complicated, and that if Anton Reitz had left his family back in Germany, he might have felt that he had a good reason to do so. I know that even today some people leave their home countries with the best intentions and end up living lives that are different than what they imagined they might be. Maybe they planned to send money home and eventually bring their family along with them?

But... he did not abandon his family. In fact, he brought his family with him to the United States. Anton Reitz, his wife, and two daughters, traveled together to the United States and

arrived in 1872.

Look for small clues that might verify or contradict your family story

When I heard the story about Anton Reitz and his "first" family, I regarded it as an interesting story that was likely untrue. I had already built my family tree on this line and I felt like it was fairly complete. I had not seen any evidence of any descendants of Anton's supposed first marriage, nor had I found any records or documents pertaining to it.

When Ancestry DNA did their recent ethnicity estimate update, however, I was intrigued by some of the changes and it led me to take a fresh look at my tree. It is clear that I have a fairly recent ancestor from Scandinavia, and I began to wonder if perhaps it was through Anton Reitz' line that this ancestry came into my DNA.

Of course, I did not learn what I actually set out to learn, but I did learn something interesting about the family story that Richard told me.

There were two clues about Anton that gave me pause and caused me to investigate whether or not he really did have a family before he married Charles' mother:

Anton was about 38 years old when he died a few months before Charles was born. By 1880 standards, that is old to be just starting a family. I don't really know for sure, but it seems likely that most men would have married well before their late 30's.

On the 1880 census (before Charles was born), Charles' mother, who had already been widowed twice, is listed as living with Anton and several other children. The kids all have different last names, but there was a girl listed by the last name of Reitz who was born when Charles' mother would have been married to someone else (i.e. not Anton Reitz). It did not make sense to me at the time, but I assumed that maybe it was a mistake.

By checking into the daughter who was listed on the census as being born in Germany (clue!), I learned the truth of the situation. I was able to locate a passenger list that showed

Anton, a wife, and two daughters leaving Bremen, Germany and arriving in New York City. The youngest daughter's age and name was a perfect match to the daughter who was listed on the 1880 census as living with Anton. It made perfect sense to me, now that I realized that this daughter was Anton's daughter that he brought to the marriage with my great-great-great grandmother.

Some family stories have sad endings

I had figured out that the family story did have some truth to it. Yes, Anton had been married in Germany, but he had not abandoned his family like his descendants believed. I had to figure out what happened to his first wife and their daughters.

First, I continued my search into what happened to the girl listed in the 1880 census. Sadly, she passed away when she was only 17 years old. Her youngest half-brother, Charles, was barely five years old. Maybe she had been sick for a while and he did not remember her, which could explain why Charles never mentioned anything about her to his grandson, Richard.

Once I learned about her fate, I thought I would see if I could find out what happened to her mother and oldest sister. Unfortunately, I found death records for them, too. The whole family crossed the Atlantic together in search of the American dream. Anton Reitz first lost his daughter, then his first wife. He married, started a new family and brought his last remaining child along, only to die himself a few years later.

And his daughter, the one born in Germany, saw her whole family pass away. She died, too, before she even reached adulthood and could start a family of her own.

While I am glad that I now know the truth about this story, the tragic ending did make me long for the time when I thought it was possible that we did have cousins somewhere in Germany who might be wondering whether they have American cousins searching for them.

Put yourself in your ancestor's shoes

Try to imagine "out of the box" places to look for records about your ancestors. Put yourself in your family members' shoes and take a mental walk through their world.

Who did they interact with? What was their profession? What type of paper trail would they have left while going about their lives?

Some of the more unique records I've seen are elementary school records, a liquor license application my great-great grandfather submitted for his saloon, and a handwritten affidavit from my fifth great-grandmother as part of a bounty-land warrant application to receive land due to her as the widow of a Revolutionary War veteran.

REMEMBER

- "Become" your ancestor to think like he/she did
- Who and what was important to them?

Search wide in your family tree

We discussed building a "wide" family tree in a previous chapter. A wide family tree is a sign of an experienced genealogist.

A wide family tree is a complete family tree that includes people who we are not descended from, and it includes their descendants. These individuals are most certainly related to us, and we can further our research goals by including them in our tree.

In other words, do not ignore your ancestor's siblings and their descendants.

I wrote more on this in another location in this book, but this is such an important topic that it deserves an additional mention. When I first got started in genealogy, I typically ignored my ancestor's siblings. Then, I realized that I was making a huge mistake and missing out on a lot of information. You never know if your ancestor was living with one of their children, or even grandchildren, from whom you are not descended, and if you do not research everyone in their family, you might miss out.

If we should include our ancestors' siblings, is there anyone else we should add to our tree? Indeed, we should add their siblings' children, grandchildren, great-grandchildren, and even great-great grandchildren.

The benefits of building a wide family tree are real and great.

Use Your DNA matches to help you add lines to your tree

You can use your DNA match list to help you figure out who other descendants of your ancestors are. Using family tree information from your matches can help you build your tree even further back – how cool is that?

While ethnicity estimates are fun and can occasionally reveal something previously unknown about our heritage, when it comes to building a family tree, our DNA match list is the most valuable tool that we have at our disposal.

Your closest DNA matches can provide information about your most recent ancestors

I always recommend that everyone use information from the closest DNA matches to "verify" our most recent ancestry. This is true for both beginning researchers and those experienced genealogists who know a lot about their family.

If we do not have our grandparents and great-grandparents listed accurately in our family trees, then any research in generations further back might be flawed.

Basically, imagine that you are building a house. The foundation must be stable, and each layer of bricks that you add to your house must add stability. The same is true for building an amazing family tree.

Once you feel confident about your recent ancestors being your biological ancestors, you are ready to take a look at your more distant cousins. When I say "more distant" I mean, specifically, your DNA matches that are estimated to be related to you at a second cousin distance to a fifth cousin distance.

How to Find Your Ancestors for Free

CHAPTER EIGHT

How to Find Your Ancestors for Free

Do you want to know how to look up your ancestors for free? In this chapter, I will teach you ways to find information about your ancestors without having to pay for a subscription.

It seems like every online records website wants to charge a hefty monthly fee. While some of those sites can be worth the investment, paying subscription fees on multiple sites can really add up over time.

I love genealogy so much, and I want to help you be able to learn about your ancestors without putting too much pressure on your monthly budget. There are multiple ways to get started finding free records and documents pertaining to your ancestors. Every single detail that you learn about your ancestors will help you piece together your family story.

Top websites for free genealogy records

Below, find my favorite websites for finding free information for family tree research.

- **Familysearch.org** This website is a completely free site managed by The Church of Jesus Christ of Latter-day Saints (also known as LDS). You will need to create a free account to access records, but it is worth it because you can find millions of records from all over the world on this site.

- **Findagrave.com** This free, volunteer-run, website contains information from volunteers about almost two hundred million graves and memorials. You can search here to find your ancestors and their family members, which is a great way to learn more about their lives and deaths.

- **WikiTree** A free website where you can look up your ancestors to see if they show up in other people's family trees. This is a cool way to see what other people have already discovered about your ancestors!

If your ancestors immigrated to the United States in the 19th or early 20th centuries, you might be able to find information about them on the Ellis Island or Castle Garden sites, completely for free.

Creative ways to find out about your ancestors for free online

There are lots of places to look for digitized records pertaining to your ancestors that you might not think to look. The following website might help you locate United States genealogy records:

US GenWeb Project A free website that serves as a directory with links to state and county records, as well as links to other free genealogy resources. It is worth checking out!

Have you considered that your ancestors may have been written about in newspapers during their life? Whether due to mundane activities like a sale of a property, or something more scandalous like being accused of a crime, we can often locate people from our family tree in old newspapers.

Fortunately, Google has put together an archive that we can search for free. It's called the Google News Archive.

If you have African-American heritage, you might want to check out the Africana Heritage Project (africanheritage.org), which is a collection of links and resources dedicated to helping the descendants of enslaved individuals document the lives of their ancestors. The site is currently undergoing a major upgrade, but you can still access the original site by clicking on a link on the homepage.

People with Jewish heritage might be able to find out more about their Jewish ancestors on the JewishGen site (jewishgen.org). This site offers records and specific information about Jewish communities in towns and locales all over the world. You will also find links to helpful resources.

Have you ever wondered if you might be able to find photographs of your ancestors? Apart from the usual places to look, you might want to check out the following site where people have uploaded genealogical photos of their ancestors:

- Dead Fred: genealogical photo archive

Are all genealogy records available for free online?

When I first began researching genealogy online, I thought that if I put my super-sleuth Google skills to use in just the right way, I would be able to find every document pertaining to my ancestors. I was convinced that they had to be out there somewhere, digitized, and ready for me to find.

Unfortunately, not every record is available online, and not every available record online can be accessed for free. I have found two subscriptions to be worth the investment, as they have saved me lots of time:

- Ancestry.com
- Newspapers.com

Definitely consider signing up for the free trials available on those sites in order to see if they work for you!

Break the Brick Walls in Your Tree

CHAPTER NINE

Break the Brick Walls in Your Tree

Are you stuck on a line of your family tree? Do you feel like your ancestor must have just appeared out of nowhere? In this chapter, learn some of the most effective genealogy strategies for breaking down "brick walls".

I have never met a genealogist, no matter how experienced, who has not encountered a dead end in their family tree. It happens to all of us, and it is incredibly frustrating when it does. It is especially frustrating when the brick wall is only a few generations back, and we feel like we should be easily able to locate records pertaining to our ancestors.

This list was compiled in order to give you ideas and inspiration about where and how to continue your search. Sometimes, a fresh perspective is necessary to regroup and begin your family tree research with a new vision of how to move forward.

Below is my go-to list for breaking down brick walls in my family tree. While I still have a few ancestors that have proven to be especially elusive, I have found every single tip to be useful in my own search.
145

I hope that you get some ideas and that you are successful in your research.

Talk to family members…. AGAIN

Talking to your family members is a great way to start your research, but it is also a great way to continue your genealogy work. When you talk to a family member you have already spoken with, be sure to let them know what you have learned about the ancestor you are interested in.

These details might jog their memory, leading them to reveal something that they had forgotten to tell you before.

I cannot stress how important it is to talk to your family members, especially the older ones, more than once. Their personal memories of people and subjects you are interested in are invaluable, and we have a limited time to document this history.

Get back to basics

Take an honest look at your ancestor and what you have already learned. Starting with the most basic details about their life, write them down.

- What is missing?
- Do you know what they did for a living?
- Who they married?
- How many children they had?

By starting from the beginning and just looking for the basics of their life story, you might find a place where you can do more research. This might lead to the information that you are looking for and help you break your brick wall.

> **REMEMBER**
>
> - We are often missing basic information
> - Start from the beginning of their story to see what you have missed

Compare notes with other relatives researching the same ancestor

The further back your ancestor is in your family tree, the more likely it is that there are other descendants or relatives who are also researching the same person. By reaching out to those individuals, you can compare notes and theories and get ideas about how to move forward.

You can find these interested parties by searching for family trees that contain your ancestor's name on websites like Ancestry and Family Search.

Start a family newsletter

Have you ever wanted to compile what you have learned into an update for your family? This is a great way to let everyone know what you have been working on without having to give separate updates to each interested person.

This is such a creative idea, and I have to admit that it is not originally mine. I have a distant cousin who started a newsletter about an ancestor that we, along with several other relatives, share in common.

About twice a year, she would send out updates on her search. This newsletter was so effective that she was contacted by other relatives that had additional information to share with her.

There are many benefits to a "family research newsletter" unique to your family's story, and I love this idea so much.

Re-examine records

Taking a second, third, or even a fourth look at a record can sometimes lead us to discover an important detail that we previously overlooked. Additionally, we might have new information that could allow us to view the original record in a new light.

For example, years ago, I sent off to the New Jersey vital records department requesting information about a great-great-uncle. On his birth certificate, the name of a witness was listed. The witness seemed like a complete stranger to me, so I ignored the name. After a couple of years, I came across a new record where a woman was listed that had the same first name as the woman on the birth certificate. These women were one and the same.

However, I did not realize this until I took a second and third look at the original record. It turns out that the surname on the birth record was the witness's married name, and I was able to research her and discover more about my ancestor in the process.

Look at old maps

Something that we should always do when we are researching our ancestors is examine maps relevant to the places where they lived. The internet is a great resource for old maps. You can find old maps of counties, states and countries. A simple Google search will often reveal the maps that you are looking for, and you can usually find them without having to pay a subscription.

By researching old maps, you will notice that names of countries, states, towns, and even streets have changed. This information can provide additional clues about what to look for in the future.

In addition, we can also get a better of idea of how far away our ancestors lived from the nearest big cities, and the names of other nearby towns where they may have moved to or where they may have married.

Put yourself in the shoes of an immigrant

Genealogists commonly get stuck on the "immigrant ancestor", since language and geographical barriers, our ancestors' poverty, and any other number of factors create additional obstacles to research.

If you put yourself in your immigrant ancestor's shoes, however, and try to think about their priorities, concerns, and social network, you might be able to find out more about them.

For example, it is safe to say that most immigrants arrive in a new country or move to a new city because they have a family member or close friend who is already living there. This friend or family member can provide valuable resources, such as a job or place to live, to help the immigrant get established in the new city.

Additionally, many immigrants established themselves in communities of immigrants who shared cultural and linguistic ties. When members of these communities moved outside of the main city, many others followed.

Pay close attention to any detail that can lead you to discover why they may have immigrated, and who their connection in their new country might have been. You might discover these details as neighbors listed on census records or fellow travelers on passenger manifests.

Check the newspaper

Newspapers are an important source of information about our ancestors.

When I first began genealogy research, I undervalued the potential of the local newspaper. I assumed that most of my ancestors had never done anything of note and I would not find articles written about them.

Oh, how wrong I was!

I have had great fun researching my ancestors on sites like Newspapers.com and have found some incredible information about people in my family tree. As it turns out, what was "newsworthy" in previous decades or centuries is different than what we might see in the daily paper today.

Historically, newspapers, especially local ones, looked more like social media posts. You could even find out who spent Saturday afternoon at whose house, if you are lucky.

And any little detail, no matter how seemingly insignificant, can help.

Whether or not our ancestors may have been mentioned in a newspaper article depends on many factors, but it is always worth your time to check to see if you can learn anything new from newspaper sources.

Check the phone book or directory

Since it has probably been several years since you last used a telephone book, our most recent equivalent to a city directory, you may not immediately think of checking these types of records to search for your ancestors.

Back in the old days, phone books and directories were useful and widely distributed. People in towns and cities depended on these compilations of residents in order to locate friends, family members, vendors and businesses to patronize.

For many people, it was a matter of pride to be listed in the city directory. There is a lot of information listed in these directories, and you also might be able to find other relatives with the same surname.

Directories are often organized in alphabetical order, which means that you will find lists of people with identical or similar surnames living in the same area. You may even notice that some of these people are living at the same address, which most likely means that they are related in some way.

We also may find people listed in directories along with their occupation, which can help us make sure that we have located the correct individual.   If we have, then we can make note of their address, which can often lead to additional record discoveries.

Do not depend on the index record – view original image

Indexes of records are easily searchable, often digitized, lists of original documents. Typically, indexes only record information that can make the record identifiable to someone who is using the index to help them locate the original record. In other words, the basic function of an index of vital records, for example, would be to help us identify our ancestor and then you can request or view the original record.

It is so easy to quickly add information from the index of a record to a family tree and move on to the next detail or relative. If there is an original image to view or request, I highly recommend doing it because indexes usually contain only the basics from a record. More often than not, there are other details recorded in the original record that are not in the index. Sometimes, this might mean ordering an original copy of a document from a repository. If this is something that you can afford to do, it might save you lots of time, and even money, in the future.

If you never view the original document, you miss out on the chance to see everything that is on the record.

Track down witnesses

Any name on the records or documents of your ancestor can have the potential to be important. This is why it is good to do some initial research on any witness that you find on a document or certificate in order to determine their relationship to your ancestor. While they might be an employee of the courthouse, they may have been a neighbor or family-in-law. They might have even been a good friend from the "old country". If you research the witness, you might discover their address. The address may lead to you realizing that they were neighbors of your ancestor.

This discovery could lead you to find out that they are first cousins, sharing a common grandparent. Perhaps this cousin of your ancestor is included in an online family tree somewhere, helping you to uncover the names of your ancestors a few more generations back.

At the very least, learning about the witnesses on your ancestors' documents – especially church records – can help you understand more about their lives. For many of us genealogists, this is our goal.

Research the cemetery

Most people do not get excited when thinking about cemeteries. That is, of course, unless you are a genealogist.

Genealogists realize that cemeteries are one of the most valuable resources for information about our families. In many cultures, the place where people are buried are often chosen because of their proximity to the burial places of other loved ones. If you are able to locate where your ancestor or relative was buried, you might be able to find additional relatives who were buried in the same cemetery.

For example, when I researched the cemetery where my grandfather was buried, I found lots of other relatives nearby. Some of the relatives were people who I knew about, but others were cousins with whom I was not familiar.

If you do not know where your ancestor was buried, but you are able to locate where some of their children were interred, this is an important clue. Check all of those cemeteries to potentially find more relatives.

You can use *Find a Grave* to do this quickly and easily. There are many other free gravestone or cemetery search sites on the internet, and I highly recommend using them to learn more about where, and with whom, your ancestors were buried.

Do not ignore image-only records

We all love a good index based on digitized records, right? Of course. Indexes make our lives and our research easier. We can quickly identify the record that corresponds to our ancestor, add the details to our records, and move on to the next research goal.

Even though indexes are great, there are millions upon millions of records that have been scanned and uploaded to sites around the world with no corresponding searchable index. Sometimes, index-only databases are in a queue, waiting for volunteers to begin the process of indexing. Other times, there are no immediate plans to index the records due to limited funds and staff.

No matter whether records are indexed, they are always valuable. Even though it might take lots of extra time, you might benefit from searching through image-only records one by one. If you choose to search through image-only records, the best strategy is to choose the records location wisely in order to maximize the possibility that you will find something of interest to you.

You can find index-only records on websites like *Family Search.*

There are lots of other places to look for image-only records, however. This is especially true for records located in other countries.

Go to church

Call or visit the church where your ancestor attended, or likely attended. They may still have records pertaining to religious ceremonies performed hundreds of years ago. If they do not hold those records on their premise, they have often been archived at a central location.

If you do not know the religion of your ancestors, then try to find out what religion they may have belonged to. Sometimes, it might be as easy as researching the community where they lived. Perhaps all, or most, residents of their local community belonged to a particular church. In addition, certain religions are more common in some countries than in others, and you can use these details to narrow down possibilities.

Once you know the religion of your ancestor, you can research the local churches in the area where they lived. These churches may be able to provide you with records or tell you where those records are being held. Religious records are often more complete than civil records, even if they are recording a similar event. For example, church marriage records might contain detailed information about the parents of the bride and groom.

Find living descendants online

If you are outgoing and a determined researcher, you might want to research people with the same surname as your ancestor who still live in the original home town. Who knows what you will learn?

Social media is a great place for this. You also could try Google. I have done this to find relatives in the Netherlands who still live in my ancestor's town of origin. I just typed in the surname and the name of the hometown.

Doing this, I found a cousin with my target ancestor's last name who was a firefighter in the town where my ancestor lived. I sent him an e-mail and it turns out that he had always wondered what had become of his American cousins who were descended from the brother of his grandfather who had come to live in the US.

Using this same strategy, I also discovered that my great-great grandmother's hometown in Slovakia, now uninhabited, is used as a demonstration town to show schoolchildren how people used to live in the old days.

There is so much left to learn about our ancestors and their lives!

Research brothers and sisters of target ancestor

We often spend a lot of time thinking only about our ancestor. This is actually a very common mistake, and I will explain why almost every new genealogist commits this error at some point during their research.

If we can figure out who our ancestor's siblings were, we can add them to our tree, as I mentioned earlier. While we are at it, we should also add the children of our ancestor's siblings to our tree. Once we know the names of these individuals, we should dedicate the same time and attention to learning about them as we have with our direct ancestor. If we do, we might find important details that can teach us about our ancestor.

For example, you might find that your ancestor was being cared for in his old age by a granddaughter who you did not even know about. Alternatively, you might find that it is easier to research the birth location of your ancestor's sibling, leading you to discover the parents of your ancestor.

171

We can also discover research partners, our distant cousins, who are interested in researching the same person. Working together on a mystery is fun and often more effective than solo research, and you can even create lasting relationships.

Conclusion

I hope that this guide has given you the motivation and knowledge necessary to build your family tree. In addition, I genuinely want the experience to be fun and entertaining for you.

As a reader of my book, you can always contact me at mercedes@whoareyoumadeof.com to ask questions and get advice about your research goals.

In addition, do not forget to visit my website, *whoareyoumadeof.com*, where you will find hundreds of helpful articles about genealogy and DNA topics.

www.ingramcontent.com/pod-product-compliance
Lightning Source LLC
Chambersburg PA
CBHW051449250726
48655CB00001B/321